A TRUE BOOK™

W9-BYA-492

Running for Public Office

SARAH DE CAPUA

Children's Press®
An Imprint of Scholastic Inc.
New York Toronto London Auckland Sydney
Mexico City New Delhi Hong Kong
Danbury, Connecticut

Content Consultant
Margaret Heubeck
Youth Leadership Initiative Director of Instruction
University of Virginia Center for Politics
Charlottesville, Virginia

Library of Congress Cataloging-in-Publication Data

De Capua, Sarah.
  Running for public office/by Sarah De Capua.
      p. cm.—(A true book)
  Includes bibliographical references and index.
  ISBN 978-0-531-26041-8 (library binding) — ISBN 978-0-531-26213-9 (pbk.)
1. Political campaigns—United States—Juvenile literature. 2. Campaign management—United
States—Juvenile literature. 3. Elections—United States—Juvenile literature. I. Title.
  JK2281.D4 2012
  324.70973—dc23   2012011308

All rights reserved. Published in 2013 by Children's Press, an imprint of Scholastic Inc.
Printed in China 62
SCHOLASTIC, CHILDREN'S PRESS, A TRUE BOOK ™, and associated logos are trademarks and/or
registered trademarks of Scholastic Inc.
2 3 4 5 6 7 8 9 10 R 22 21 20 19 18 17 16 15 14

**Front cover: Candidate
holding a "Vote" button**

**Back cover: Republican (left) and
Democratic (right) party symbols**

Find the Truth!

Everything you are about to read is true *except* for one of the sentences on this page.

Which one is **TRUE**?

T or F Not all campaign workers are paid.

T or F Candidates for public office never campaign on Election Day.

Find the answers in this book.

Contents

THE **BIG** TRUTH!

Being Part of a Party

New members of the U.S. House of Representatives are sworn into public office.

4 The Road to the Presidency

5 Election Day

The elephant symbolizes the Republican Party. The donkey stands for the Democratic Party.

5

The president is the most recognizable public officeholder in the United States.

Serving the Public

Have you ever seen the president give a speech? Have you heard adults talk about the mayor, Congress, or the school board? The president, the mayor, and members of Congress and the school board are all public officeholders. Their decisions affect all of a community's members, whether it is a small town or the entire United States.

The U.S. president can only be elected to the presidency twice.

Choosing Our Leaders

The United States is a republic with strong democratic traditions. Citizens in a republic do not run the government directly. They choose leaders to make decisions on the public's behalf. These public officeholders are chosen through elections. People vote for the candidates they believe will best represent the community's interests.

The first U.S. president elected by secret ballot was Grover Cleveland in 1892.

Citizens in the United States vote by secret ballot.

Voters in some areas elect the local school board members. In other places, an elected authority, such as the mayor, appoints the members.

Many Different Offices

Public officeholders have a variety of responsibilities. Executives, or leaders, include town and city mayors, state governors, and the U.S. president. Some officeholders are responsible for supporting these elected leaders. Cabinet members are officeholders who advise the president or governor. Local and state boards of commissioners serve similar purposes in their governments. The public elects some of these people. Others, such as the secretary of state and other cabinet members, are appointed.

Judges usually begin their careers as lawyers.

Members of the state legislature and federal Congress are also public officeholders. These senators and representatives are the government's lawmakers. Other officeholders work in the justice system. District attorneys, attorneys general, and other lawyers represent the government's interests in legal battles. They might be appointed or elected, depending on the rules of the community they represent. Judges—from those who preside over local courts to members of the U.S. Supreme Court—are also either appointed or elected.

Many places have sheriffs. These men and women are elected to lead a county's law enforcement. Local, state, and federal treasurers are elected to keep track of the government's money. Commissioners of revenue and tax collectors make sure community members pay their taxes. Medical examiners, also called coroners, might be elected or appointed. These officeholders investigate the causes of certain suspicious deaths in their state or county. Sometimes, the coroner also holds another office, such as district attorney.

A sheriff is usually voted into office for three to four years.

11

Meeting the Qualifications

All occupations have qualifications a person must meet before taking the job. Public offices are no different. Most officeholders must be at least 18 years old. Governors, state senators, and state representatives are often required to be at least 25 to 30 years old. Members of the U.S. Congress have similar age requirements. The U.S. president must be at least 35 years old. Some positions, including judges and some medical examiners, also require special education or training.

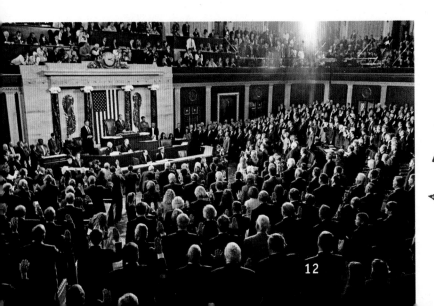

A U.S. representative must be at least 25 years old.

Immigrants who gain U.S. citizenship are called naturalized citizens.

Officeholders should be residents in the town, county, state, or nation they represent. They must also be U.S. citizens. For most offices, it doesn't matter whether they were born citizens or became citizens after moving to the country. However, the U.S. president must be born in the United States.

Anyone can run for office if he or she meets the qualifications. It is each person's right as a U.S. citizen.

CINDY FOR CONG

Campaigns generally have a headquarters from which activities are run.

CHAPTER 2

Kicking Off the Campaign

Running for public office is a big decision. A candidate should be committed to the causes and the community that he or she wishes to represent. A **campaign** for public office is also a huge commitment of time and energy. Running a campaign requires organizing volunteers, raising funds, and convincing people that the candidate is the right person for the job.

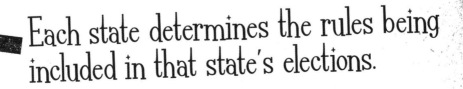

Each state determines the rules being included in that state's elections.

Getting Started

To run for office, candidates must first visit the local elections clerk for a **petition** form. Filling out this form ensures that a candidate's name will appear on election **ballots**. A certain number of voters need to sign a petition. City officeholders often need fewer than 100 signatures. Offices that serve larger communities need more signatures. U.S. House of Representatives candidates need 2,298 signatures to get on the ballot. U.S. Senate and presidential candidates need more than 100,000.

Signers include their names and addresses when they sign a petition.

Volunteers in the community sometimes hold fund-raisers to support their favorite candidate.

Gathering Resources

It costs money to run for office. When candidates file petitions at the elections clerk's office, they sometimes have to pay a fee. This fee ranges from a few hundred to a few thousand dollars. In addition, candidates need to pay for a space where they can set up headquarters. Making and distributing commercials, signs, and other advertisements costs money, too. Contributions might come from individual supporters, businesses, and other organizations. Some candidates also contribute their own money.

Campaign information is distributed in many forms. Signs, brochures, and door hangers are just a few examples.

A successful campaign needs people as well. Many of these people are volunteers who help out for free. Volunteers might stuff envelopes with information, distribute signs and brochures, call or visit voters, and help keep the headquarters organized. Anyone who supports a candidate can volunteer. Other campaign workers are paid, including campaign managers, Web designers, and writers. These professionals often have years of experience working for candidates and officeholders.

Managing the Campaign

After the candidate, the campaign manager is perhaps the most important person in a campaign. Campaign managers have the full-time job of executing a campaign **strategy** and managing all the people and activities involved in running for office. They organize events, keep track of public opinion, and solve any problems that may arise. Taking care of these things leaves a candidate free to visit with voters and gain support.

Journalists from newspapers, Web sites, and television news programs might publish interviews with candidates.

CHAPTER 3

Getting the Word Out

The need to convince people to vote for a particular candidate lies at the heart of every campaign. Voters must be made familiar with a candidate's name and his or her opinions on important issues. There are a number of ways to spread the word about a candidate. Some methods work better for certain types of campaigns than others, but all candidates use a variety of strategies.

Candidates may call press conferences to make important public announcements.

21

Local and state candidates often walk door-to-door to talk with voters.

Meeting with Voters

Candidates can meet directly with voters. A candidate might walk door-to-door, visiting voters in their homes. People running for higher offices, such as Congress or the presidency, often don't have time to do this personally, so volunteers take over. Meetings in a supporter's home or at a town hall allow candidates to talk to a relatively small group of voters. They can discuss important issues and their plans after taking office.

Rallies are huge meetings that are usually held outside or in large indoor spaces, such as stadiums or school auditoriums. Hundreds or even thousands of voters gather together to support and learn more about a candidate. Celebrities, business leaders, or other politicians often give speeches. Then the candidate speaks. He or she will often shake hands with voters before or after the speech. Sometimes, news reporters can ask the candidate questions.

The candidate is always the last to deliver a speech at rallies.

Advertising

Commercials help inform voters about a candidate's position on certain issues. Ads might quickly highlight a candidate's strengths or point out possible problems in an opponent's campaign. Television and radio are common places to find commercials. These ads usually last about 30 seconds. Candidates often publish ads in newspapers and on the Internet, too.

Candidates often say a few sentences in their commercials.

Campaign Web sites often include videos, biographies, photos, and a schedule of upcoming campaign events.

The Internet offers candidates another way to connect with voters. Candidates can set up campaign Web sites, YouTube channels, Facebook pages, and Twitter accounts. Voters can use these tools to learn more about a candidate's background, opinions on important issues, and upcoming events. On many of these Web sites, voters can also ask questions and send feedback to candidates.

Volunteers walking door-to-door often have a list of people who might be swayed to vote for their candidate.

Candidates do not have to depend on technology. Whether a campaign is big or small, letters and brochures are often sent to voters with information on a candidate. These might come through the mail or be dropped off by the candidate or volunteers walking door-to-door. Candidates can also put up ads on billboards along highways to attract the attention of drivers.

Showing Support

Voters can help spread the word for their favorite candidate. Have you ever seen campaign signs in yards or windows? These have a candidate's name in big letters and usually include the office the candidate hopes to win and the year of the election. Supporters can also put bumper stickers on their cars and wear buttons with their candidate's name. These items can be obtained at a campaign's local office or at events such as rallies.

Buttons often become collector's items after campaigns are over.

Being Part of a Party

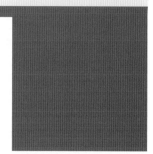

Political parties help candidates raise money, run campaigns, and define goals while in office. Most people who run for public office belong to either the Democratic or Republican Party. Other candidates belong to smaller parties, often called third parties. Candidates might also run as independents and not belong to any party.

The Republican Party is sometimes called the GOP, or Grand Old Party. Republicans generally believe in limiting the power of the federal government, especially in business.

Some of the most powerful third parties today are the Libertarian, Reform, and Green parties. Third parties rarely gain as much attention as the Democratic and Republican parties do, but their campaigns can affect government decisions even when their candidates do not win.

Democrats generally believe in a federal government with more power over business and often support aid programs for the unemployed, the elderly, and other groups.

Republican candidate Mitt Romney officially began his presidential campaign about a year and a half before the 2012 election.

The Road to the Presidency

It can be a long, difficult road for anyone running for a public office. However, the road to the presidency is probably the longest and most difficult. Campaigns for a local office, such as mayor, might last a few months. Campaigns for higher offices, such as senator or representative, can last a year or longer. But campaigns for the U.S. presidency generally begin more than two years before Election Day.

Presidential campaigns include millions of volunteer workers.

Earning the Nomination

A person who wants to run as a Democratic or Republican presidential candidate must first win the party's **nomination**. Nominees are chosen through a series of primary elections or, in some states, **caucuses**. Local or state governments organize a state's primary. The political parties are in charge of holding caucuses. In both, people vote for the person they believe should run for president within a certain party.

Timeline of Public Offices

500 BCE

Ancient Greeks are among the first people to vote for public officeholders.

1787 CE

The U.S. Constitution, which contains rules for conducting national elections, is signed.

The winners of these elections inform party officials which candidate has the most voter support and would therefore be most likely to win the general election. Each party's presidential nominee is announced at the party's national **convention**. Then a presidential candidate announces his or her running mate, the person chosen to run as vice president. Some third parties choose their nominees through conventions, too.

facebook

Facebook helps you connect and share with the people in your life.

1951

The Twenty-second Amendment is passed, limiting the U.S. presidency to two terms.

2004

Facebook is launched, providing a new way for users to follow their favorite candidates.

Winning Over a Nation

Because the president represents everyone in the United States, a presidential candidate's campaign covers the entire country. This requires millions of workers and millions of dollars. Campaigning begins well before the primaries and caucuses. Candidates deliver speeches and attend events in most states. They

also participate in debates. These events bring together two or more candidates, allowing them to compare opinions on important issues. Participants are asked a series of questions and take turns giving short responses.

Presidential debates might cover a range of topics or focus on one or two specific issues.

Kids Vote

Every four years, as the presidential election approaches, Scholastic, a children's book publisher, takes a **poll**. Hundreds of thousands of kids send in their votes for president, either by mail or online. The results are later published in the classroom magazines *Scholastic News* and *Junior Scholastic*. In almost every election since 1940, these polls have accurately predicted the election's winner. Next time there is a presidential election, pay attention to each of the candidates. Who would earn your vote?

Ballots often include several items on which a person can vote, including new laws and public officeholders.

CHAPTER 5

Election Day

Whether running for city council or the presidency, candidates all prepare for one day: Election Day. This is when people across the city, state, or country cast their votes. Presidential elections take place every four years on a Tuesday between November 2 and 8. Many states hold elections for senators, representatives, and others on the same day. Some elections take place in other years, depending on the town, state, and length of time an officeholder stays in office.

Last-Minute Efforts

Even on Election Day, a candidate's work continues. Candidates or volunteers might visit polling places, greeting voters in hopes of gaining additional votes. Candidates must usually conduct these greetings a certain distance away from the polling place so voters don't feel pressured as they get ready to vote. People running for state or national offices might hold events in certain cities or states. They sometimes travel thousands of miles to campaign, then return home to cast their own ballots.

Candidates or volunteers often talk to voters outside polling places.

Presidential Election Night rallies can cost millions of dollars.

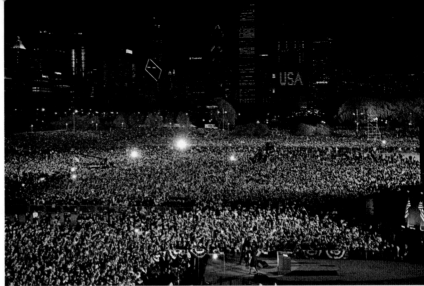

Presidential Election Night rallies can include hundreds of thousands of people.

Awaiting Results

As voting continues and ballots are counted, many candidates hold gatherings. They invite their families, campaign workers, and other supporters. After the results are announced, both the winners and losers deliver speeches. The winner discusses plans for what he or she will do while in office. Those who lost the election deliver **concession** speeches. During a concession speech, a candidate thanks all those who helped with the campaign and wishes the winner luck.

A state senator raises his hands in victory after hearing he has won his election.

The results of an election are generally known the night of or the morning after Election Day. While presidential election results are not official until Congress approves them the following January, there is often a clear winner. But this is not always the case. At times, results may come as a surprise the next day or may not even be known for weeks.

A Long Election

The 2000 presidential election took more than a month to be decided. Republican George W. Bush was running against Democrat Al Gore. Throughout the campaign, voters seemed equally divided between the candidates. Even on Election Day, there was no clear winner. In Florida, the final count was so close that the state did a recount. Both candidates took the issue to court. It was not until December 9 that the U.S. Supreme Court upheld the state recount that determined that Bush had won.

Thousands of ballots were recounted by hand following the presidential election in 2000.

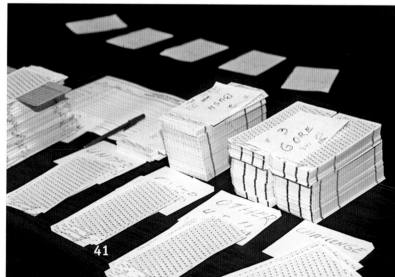

Election Surprises

Other presidential elections have had interesting results. In the 1948 election, the *Chicago Tribune* and a few other newspapers declared candidate Thomas E. Dewey the winner. In truth, Dewey had lost the election to Harry S. Truman. In 1800, presidential candidates Thomas Jefferson and Aaron Burr tied in votes. The decision was then passed to the House of Representatives. The representatives argued until the following February, when the House declared Jefferson the winner. Burr became vice president.

Newly reelected president Harry S. Truman holds up a copy of the *Chicago Tribune* declaring Thomas Dewey the election's winner.

Public officeholders are sworn in to their offices.

What Happens Next?

Winning an election is not the end of the road.
Those who win a public office go on to the difficult
job of serving the public. Even if a candidate loses
an election, there is always the next one. Many
elected officials have lost elections before winning
their seats in public office. However, win or lose,
running for office is hard work. It takes time, effort,
and serious dedication. ★

True Statistics

Section of the U.S. Constitution that explains rules for presidential elections: Article II, Section 1

Year the modern Republican Party was formed in the United States: 1854

Year the modern Democratic Party was formed in the United States: Around 1832

Year the first known law enforcing minimum age requirements for public officeholders was passed: 180 BCE, in the Roman Empire

Youngest person elected mayor in the United States: Brian Zimmerman, who was 11 years old when he was elected mayor of Crabb, Texas, in 1983

Youngest person in the world to serve as a judge: Marc Griffin, who was 17 when he became a judge in Greenwood, Indiana, in the 1970s

Did you find the truth?

T Not all campaign workers are paid.

F Candidates for public office never campaign on Election Day.

Resources

Books

Cheney, Lynne V. *We the People: The Story of Our Constitution*. New York: Simon & Schuster Books for Young Readers, 2008.

De Capua, Sarah. *Voting*. New York: Children's Press, 2013.

Nelson, Robin, and Sandy Donovan. *Getting Elected: A Look at Running for Office*. Minneapolis: Lerner Publications, 2012.

Scher, Linda, and Mary Oates Johnson. *Candidates, Campaigns & Elections: Projects, Activities, Literature Links*. New York: Scholastic/Teaching Resources, 2007.

Visit this Scholastic Web site for more information on running for public office:
★ www.factsfornow.scholastic.com
Enter the keywords **Public Office**

Important Words

ballots (BAL-uhts) — slips of paper or machines that provide a way to vote secretly

campaign (kam-PAYN) — organized action in order to achieve a particular goal

caucuses (KAW-kuhs-iz) — meetings of members of a particular political party to select candidates

concession (kuhn-SESH-uhn) — something that is allowed or agreed, often reluctantly

convention (kuhn-VEN-shuhn) — a formal gathering of people

nomination (nah-muh-NAY-shuhn) — the suggestion that someone would be a good person to do an important job

petition (puh-TISH-uhn) — a letter signed by many people asking those in power to change their policy or actions, or telling them what signers think about a certain issue, situation, or person

political parties (puh-LIT-i-kuhl PAHR-teez) — organizations that elect representatives to be candidates for government and that create or support their policies

poll (POHL) — a survey of people's opinions or beliefs

rallies (RAL-eez) — large meetings for a purpose

strategy (STRAT-i-jee) — a clever plan for achieving a goal

Index

Page numbers in **bold** indicate illustrations

About the Author

Sarah De Capua is the author of many nonfiction books for children. She enjoys helping young readers learn about our country through civics education. She has been volunteering for candidates who are running for public office since she was eight years old, so she knows that even kids can make a difference in a candidate's campaign. De Capua works as a children's book author and editor, as well as a college composition instructor. She holds a master's degree in teaching from Sacred Heart University in Connecticut, and is currently working toward her doctorate in composition and TESOL at Indiana University of Pennsylvania. She has written other True Books in this set, including *Paying Taxes, Serving on a Jury*, and *Voting*.